Pasto
W. ?
Spoka

SPI.
Empowering the New Testament Church Study Guide

STUDY GUIDE

Spiritual Gifts

EMPOWERING
the
NEW
TESTAMENT
CHURCH

GERRY PEAK

BROADMAN PRESS
NASHVILLE, TENNESSEE

Contents

Introduction

This study guide is an aid to help you understand Kenneth S. Hemphill's *Spiritual Gifts: Empowering the New Testament Church* (Broadman Press). Following the questions throughout this study guide, there are page numbers in parentheses ( ). These are the actual page numbers in the book where the answers are found. Some of the questions ask for your own personal feelings about your church or your own Christian life.

Ken Hemphill has made available an excellent exegetical study of the major gift passages in the New Testament. This study guide should be used along with Dr. Hemphill's book and the Bible.

There is an appendix entitled, "Discovering My Gift." It will help you to discover the gift God has given you. It will also encourage you to improve the gift and use it for the upbuilding of the church.

For those who like to have the Scripture printed, you will find the *New American Standard Version* of the major passages printed in this guide. It is my hope that this printing will help you study Dr. Hemphill's book with the help of this guide.

1. An Early Look at Ministry Structure

1 Thessalonians 5:12-22

[12]But we request of you, brethren, that you appreciate those who diligently labor among you, and have charge over you in the Lord and give you instruction, [13]and that you esteem them very highly in love because of their work. Live in peace with one another. [14]And we urge you, brethren, admonish the unruly, encourage the fainthearted, help the weak, be patient with all men. [15]See that no one repays another with evil for evil, but always seek after that which is good for one another and for all men. [16]Rejoice always; [17]pray without ceasing; [18]in everything give thanks; for this is God's will for you in Christ Jesus. [19]Do not quench the Spirit; [20]do not despise prophetic utterances. [21]But examine everything carefully; hold fast to that which is good; [22]abstain from every form of evil.

1. Why is a study of 1 and 2 Thessalonians important in a study of spiritual gifts? (p. 18) _____

2. What are some clues given in 1 Thessalonians and Philippians that suggest that Paul was in Thes-

salonica longer than the three Sabbaths mentioned in Acts 17:1-10? (p. 19) _____

_____

_____

3. What evidence points to Jason's home as being the center for Christian activity in Thessalonica? (pp. 19-20) _____

_____

_____

4. Why was Paul concerned about the attacks some Thessalonians had made on his character? (p. 21)

_____

_____

How did he respond to these attacks? (pp. 21-22)

_____

_____

_____

5. What are some possible reasons why Paul wrote 1 Thessalonians? (p. 23) _____

_____

_____

6. Paul's overarching desire [in 1 Thessalonians] was to establish _____ in the _____ so they could _____ one another in the face of _____ and the community could command the _____ of the _____ . (p. 26)

7. What are the three duties of the church leader (pastor) that Paul describes in 1 Thessalonians 5:12? (p. 25)
   (1) _____
   (2) _____

(3) _____

8. What negative actions were the "unruly" members committing? (p. 28) _____

_____

_____

9. If your church membership includes some "unruly" members, what do these persons do that tend to polarize people and weaken the unity of your church's fellowship? _____

_____

_____

10. Verse 14 refers to the disconsolate/fainthearted and the weak. What persons in your church would fit these descriptions? (p. 31) _____

_____

_____

11. Why is patience required in community ministry? (p. 31) _____

_____

_____

12. What alternative behavior did Paul recommend in lieu of repaying evil for evil (v. 15)? (pp. 31-32)

_____

_____

13. Evaluate a recent worship experience of your church according to the criteria Paul gave in 1 Thessalonians 5:16-18. Study a copy of the order of service if necessary. What aspect of the service contributed to rejoicing? _____

_____

to prayer? _____

_____

to giving thanks? _____

_____

14. According to the definition given in this chapter, *ecstatic* refers to (p. 34) _____

_____

15. According to the definition given in this chapter, *prophecy* refers to (p. 35) _____

_____

16. What contemporary events can tempt persons to "despise" all "prophetic utterances" today? (p. 35)

_____

_____

17. Why was Paul concerned that some Thessalonian believers were despising "prophetic" teaching? (p. 36) _____

_____

18. After examining "everything carefully," how were believers to respond to the prophetic teaching they heard (vv. 21-22)? (p. 36) _____

_____

19. Although spiritual gifts are not mentioned in 1 Thessalonians, Paul makes at least three points concerning community ministry. What are these points? (p. 38)
    (1) Every member is _____

_____

    (2) Even though all members must minister, God has _____

_____

    (3) A relationship exists between the leading of the

community and the _____

_____

20. What major truths have you learned from this chapter?

2. Identifying the Spirituals

1. Identify three problems of the church at Corinth (pp. 40-41).
   (1) _____
   (2) _____
   (3) _____
2. How long did Paul stay in Corinth (p. 42)? _____
3. Identify at least two events that occurred between Paul's visit to Corinth and the writing of 1 Corinthians (pp. 42-43).
   (1) _____
   (2) _____
4. Describe the "spirituals" of Corinth (pp. 43-52).

   _____

   _____

   _____

5. What is meant by "overrealized eschatalogy" (pp. 46-47)? _____

   _____

   _____

6. How did the spirituals use their understanding of freedom as a license for sexual immorality (p. 49)?

   _____

   _____

7. How did Paul correct the spirituals' demand for freedom at any cost (p. 49)? _____

8. Identify two ways in which Paul redefines the spiritual person (pp. 50-51).
   (1) _____
   (2) _____

3. Redefining the Spiritual Gifts

1 Corinthians 12

[1]Now concerning spiritual gifts, brethren, I do not want you to be unaware. [2]You know that when you were pagans, you were led astray to the dumb idols, however you were led. [3]Therefore I make known to you, that no one speaking by the Spirit of God says, "Jesus is accursed"; and no one can say, "Jesus is Lord," except by the Holy Spirit. [4]Now there are varieties of gifts, but the same Spirit. [5]And there are varieties of ministries, and the same Lord. [6]And there are varieties of effects, but the same God who works all things in all persons. [7]But to each one is given the manifestation of the Spirit for the common good. [8]For to one is given the word of wisdom through the Spirit, and to another the word of knowledge according to the same Spirit; [9]to another faith by the same Spirit, and to another gifts of healing by the one Spirit, [10]and to another the effecting of miracles, and to another prophecy, and to another the distinguishing of spirits, to another various kinds of tongues, and to another the interpretation of tongues. [11]But one and the same Spirit works all these things, distributing to each one individually just as He wills. [12]For even as the body is one and yet has many members, and all

the members of the body, though they are many, are one body, so also is Christ. [13]For by one Spirit we were all baptized into one body, whether Jews or Greeks, whether slaves or free, and we were all made to drink of one Spirit. [14]For the body is not one member, but many. [15]If the foot should say, "Because I am not a hand, I am not a part of the body," it is not for this reason any the less a part of the body. [16]And if the ear should say, "Because I am not an eye, I am not a part of the body," it is not for this reason any the less a part of the body. [17]If the whole body were an eye, where would the hearing be? If the whole were hearing, where would the sense of smell be? [18]But now God has placed the members, each one of them, in the body, just as He desired. [19]And if they were all one member, where would the body be? [20]But now there are many members, but one body. [21]And the eye cannot say to the hand, "I have no need of you"; or again the head to the feet, "I have no need of you." [22]On the contrary, it is much truer that the members of the body which seem to be weaker are necessary; [23]and those members of the body, which we deem less honorable, on these we bestow more abundant honor, and our unseemly members come to have more abundant seemliness, [24]whereas our seemly members have no need of it. But God has so composed the body, giving more abundant honor to that member which lacked, [25]that there should be no division in the body, but that the members should have the same care for one another. [26]And if one member suffers, all the members suffer with it; if one member is honored, all the members rejoice with it. [27]Now you are Christ's body, and individually members of it. [28]And God has appointed in the church, first apostles, second prophets, third teachers, then miracles, then gifts of healings, helps, administrations, various kinds of tongues. [29]All are not apostles, are they? All are not prophets, are they? All are not teachers, are they? All are not workers of miracles, are they? [30]All do not have gifts of healings, do they? All do not speak with tongues, do they? All do not interpret, do they? [31]But earnestly desire the greater gifts. And I show you a still more excellent way.

1. What was the question or inquiry to which Paul responded in 1 Corinthians 12—14 (p. 54)? _____

2. What is ironic about the spiritual's claim that they possessed all knowledge (pp. 54-55)? _____

3. How did Paul refute the spirituals' claim that they alone possessed the Spirit (pp. 56-57)? _____

4. Why did Paul, in 12:2, remind the Corinthians of their previous pagan life-styles (p. 57)? _____

5. Explain the significance of Paul's substituting *charismata* (manifestation of grace) for *pneumatika* (manifestation of the Spirit) (pp. 58-59)? _____

6. What was Paul's reason for excluding human boasting in 1 Corinthians 1:29 (p. 59)? _____

7. Why was Corinthian celibacy insufficient grounds for boasting (pp. 59-60)? _____

_____

8. In 12:4-6, the words *gifts, ministries,* and *effects* are used to describe gifts for ministry. Describe the perspective of each of these words (p. 60).
   GIFTS—_____
   MINISTRIES—_____
   EFFECTS— _____

9. What point is made by the repetition of *variety* and *same* in 12:4-6 (p. 60)? _____

_____

10. What two important points does Paul make in 12:7 (pp. 60-61)?
    (1) _____
    (2) _____

11. What are some possible reasons why Paul would include such a miraculous list of gifts in 12:8-10 (pp. 61-62)? _____

_____

_____

12. Why does Dr. Hemphill suggest that a more accurate title for this book would have been *Grace Gifts: Empowering the New Testament Church* (p. 63)? _____

_____

_____

13. Explain how the extended metaphor of the body in 12:12-31 supports Paul's emphasis on unity and diversity in the church (pp. 64-65)? _____

_____

_____

14. How did the spirituals' emphasis on possessing miraculous gifts ignore the need for variety (p. 65)?

_____

_____

15. Complete this sentence: "The zeal of the spirituals to _____ _____ in possessing the _____ gifts had resulted in a failure to appreciate the _____ of the _____ and in turn led to rampant _____ which caused them to act without _____ of other believers" (p. 66).

16. Explain the difference between independence and interdependence in the body of Christ (p. 67). __

_____

17. To whom is Paul referring in 12:22-24 by the words _less honorable, unseemly,_ and _weaker_ (pp. 67-68)? _____

_____

18. In what ways today are Christians guilty of treating some tasks as less honorable or unseemly (p. 69)?

_____

_____

19. Why is discord in the church disastrous (p. 69)?

_____

20. Discord in the church should be replaced by _____ _____ and _____ (p. 69).

21. How does the second gift list in 12:28 differ from the list in 12:8-10 (pp. 70-73)? _____ ____

_____

22. Why are two gift lists given in this chapter? (pp. 70-71) _____

23. What did Paul mean by "greater gifts" in 12:31 (pp. 73-74)? _____

24. What is meant by "a still more excellent way" in 12:31 (p. 74)? _____

25. How did Paul redefine spiritual gifts in chapter 12?

_____

_____

_____

4. The Spiritual Man Redefined

1 Corinthians 13

[1]If I speak with the tongues of men and of angels, but do not have love, I have become a noisy gong or a clanging cymbal. [2]And if I have the gift of prophecy, and know all mysteries and all knowledge; and if I have all faith, so as to remove mountains, but do not have love, I am nothing. [3]And if I give all my possessions to feed the poor, and if I deliver my body to be burned, but do not have love, it profits me nothing. [4]Love is patient, love is kind, and is not jealous; love does not brag and is not arrogant, [5]does not act unbecomingly; it does not seek its own, is not provoked, does not take into account a wrong suffered, [6]does not rejoice in unrighteousness, but rejoices with the truth; [7]bears all things, believes all things, hopes all things, endures all things. [8]Love never fails; but if there are gifts of prophecy, they will be done away; if there are tongues, they will cease; if there is knowledge, it will be done away. [9]For we know in part, and we prophesy in part; [10]but when the perfect comes, the partial will be done away. [11]When I was a child, I used to speak as a child, think as a child, reason as a child; when I became a man, I did away with childish things. [12]For now we see in a mirror dimly, but

then face to face; now I know in part, but then I shall know fully just as I also have been fully known. ¹³But now abide faith, hope, love, these three; but the greatest of these is love.

1. Complete this sentence: "Love is the _____ that one is an authentic _____ person" (p. 77).

2. To what might Paul be referring when he wrote of "the tongues . . . of angels" in 13:1 (pp. 77-78)?

   _____

   _____

3. In 13:3, Paul contrasted giving away possessions and giving up his body to be burned with what negative ascetic practices of the Corinthians? (pp. 80-81) __

   _____

   _____

4. According to 13:4-8, list the things that Paul says love is and is not (pp. 81-86).
   Love is _____
   Love is not _____

   _____

   _____

5. According to the list in 4. above, what can be concluded about the behavior of the spirituals (pp. 81-86)? _____

   _____

   _____

6. Look at the list in 4. above. Which of these behaviors are you most likely to demonstrate in your life?

   _____

   _____

   _____

7. Describe the contrast Paul makes in 13:8-13 of an eternal love and the partial (overrealized eschatalogy). (pp. 86-87) _____

    _____

    _____

8. Verse 10 refers to "when the perfect comes." Explain what Paul means by *perfect*. (pp. 87-88) _____

    _____

    _____

9. What does Dr. Hemphill mean when he writes, "Gifts do not possess any *sign* value, they possess only *service* value"? (p. 90) _____

    _____

    _____

5. The Spiritual Person Seeking Spiritual Gifts

1 Corinthians 14

[1]Pursue love, yet desire earnestly spiritual gifts, but especially that you may prophesy. [2]For one who speaks in a tongue does not speak to men, but to God; for no one understands, but in his spirit he speaks mysteries. [3]But one who prophesies speaks to men for edification and exhortation and consolation. [4]One who speaks in a tongue edifies himself; but one who prophesies edifies the church. [5]Now I wish that you all spoke in tongues, but even more that you would prophesy; and greater is one who prophesies than one who speaks in tongues, unless he interprets, so that the church may receive edifying. [6]But now, brethren, if I come to you speaking in tongues, what shall I profit you, unless I speak to you either by way of revelation or of knowledge or of prophecy or of teaching? [7]Yet even lifeless things, either flute or harp, in producing a sound, if they do not produce a distinction in the tones, how will it be known what is played on the flute or on the harp? [8]For if the bugle produces an indistinct sound, who will prepare himself for battle? [9]So also you, unless you utter by the tongue speech that is clear, how will it be known what is spoken? For you will be speaking into the air. [10]There

are, perhaps, a great many kinds of languages in the world, and no kind is without meaning. [11]If then I do not know the meaning of the language, I shall be to the one who speaks a barbarian, and the one who speaks will be a barbarian to me. [12]So also you, since you are zealous of spiritual gifts, seek to abound for the edification of the church. [13]Therefore let one who speaks in a tongue pray that he may interpret. [14]For if I pray in a tongue, my spirit prays, but my mind is unfruitful. [15]What is the outcome then? I shall pray with the spirit and I shall pray with the mind also; I shall sing with the spirit and I shall sing with the mind also. [16]Otherwise if you bless in the spirit only, how will the one who fills the place of the ungifted say the "Amen" at your giving of thanks, since he does not know what you are saying? [17]For you are giving thanks well enough, but the other man is not edified. [18]I thank God, I speak in tongues more than you all; [19]however, in the church I desire to speak five words with my mind, that I may instruct others also, rather than ten thousand words in a tongue. [20]Brethren, do not be children in your thinking; yet in evil be babes, but in your thinking be mature. [21]In the Law it is written, "By men of strange tongues and by the lips of strangers I will speak to this people, and even so they will not listen to Me," says the Lord. [22]So then tongues are for a sign, not to those who believe, but to unbelievers; but prophecy is for a sign, not to unbelievers, but to those who believe. [23]If therefore the whole church should assemble together and all speak in tongues, and ungifted men or unbelievers enter, will they not say that you are mad? [24]But if all prophesy, and an unbeliever or an ungifted man enters, he is convicted by all, he is called to account by all; [25]the secrets of his heart are disclosed; and so he will fall on his face and worship God, declaring that God is certainly among you. [26]What is the outcome then, brethren? When you assemble, each one has a psalm, has a teaching, has a revelation, has a tongue, has an interpretation. Let all things be done for edification. [27]If anyone speaks in a tongue, it should be by two or at the most three, and each in turn, and let one interpret; [28]but if there is no interpreter, let him keep silent in the church; and let him speak to himself and to God. [29]And let two or three prophets speak, and let the others pass judgment. [30]But if a revelation is made to another who is seated, let the first keep silent. [31]For you can all prophesy one by one, so that all may learn and all may be exhorted; [32]and the spirits of prophets are subject to prophets; [33]for God is not a God of confusion but of peace, as in all the churches of the saints. [34]Let the women keep silent in the churches; for they are not permitted to speak, but let them subject themselves, just as the Law also says. [35]And if they desire to learn anything, let them ask their own husbands at home; for it is improper for a woman to speak in church. [36]Was it from you that the word of God first went forth? Or has it come to you only? [37]If anyone thinks he is a prophet or spiritual, let him recognize that the things which I write to you are the Lord's commandment. [38]But if anyone does not recognize this, he is not recognized. [39]Therefore, my brethren, desire earnestly to prophesy, and do not forbid to speak in tongues. [40]But let all things be done properly and in an orderly manner.

1. How does Paul relate *love, gifts,* and *edification* in chap-

ter 14? (pp. 92-93) _____

_____

2. If gifts are distributed by the Spirit as He wills, how can Paul suggest that one should seek a certain gift, as he does in 14:1? (pp. 94-95) _____

_____

3. How does the criteria of edification and intelligibility influence whether tongues or prophecy has priority? (p. 95) _____

4. Compare the value of glossolalia in private devotions and in the gathered community of believers? (pp. 96-97) _____

_____

_____

5. If Paul's' wish in verse 5 "that you all spoke in tongues," is not to be taken at face value, what is Paul really saying? (pp. 97-98) _____

_____

6. Why is interpretation important to the value of tongues within the congregation? (pp. 97-98) ____

_____

7. What point is Paul making in 14:7-8 by alluding to the flute, harp, and bugle? (pp. 98-99) _____

_____

8. What must be the controlling factor in a person's

"seeking" a particular gift? (p. 100) _____

9. Of the gifts studied so far, which gift(s) do you desire and why? _____

_____

10. In 14:13, for what should persons who speak in tongues pray? (pp. 101-102) _____

11. What are the positives and negatives of religious ecstasy? (pp. 102-103)
Positives: _____

Negatives: _____

12. Why did Paul refrain from publicly displaying his gift of tongues? (pp. 104-105) _____

13. According to 14:22, which gift is a sign to unbelievers and which to believers? (pp. 106-107)
Sign to unbelievers: _____
Sign to believers: _____

14. What does *ungifted* (vv. 23-24) mean? (p. 107) _____

15. In verses 23-25, what two differing situations cause these opposite reactions: (a) persons thinking that you are mad, and (b) persons declaring that God is certainly among you? (p. 108) _____

_____

16. In 14:26, what gifts are mentioned and how are they

to be exercised? (pp. 109-110) _____

_____

_____

17. What might lead a person with the gift of tongues to forfeit the right to speak audibly in the assembly? (p. 112) _____

18. What evidence is found in 14:29-33 to show that the gift of prophecy was abused at Corinth? (p. 113)

_____

19. What two elements of control should always be at work when persons prophesy in the assembly? (p. 115) _____

_____

20. Based on what Paul wrote in 1 Corinthians 11, to whom is Paul referring in 14:34-35 when he writes "let the women keep silent in the churches"? (pp. 116-121) _____

_____

21. In your own words, rewrite Paul's warning to prophets and spirituals in 14:37-38: _____

_____

_____

22. How do 14:40 and 14:33 relate to creating an atmosphere in which the body of Christ may be edified?

_____

_____

_____

_____

6. Rome, a Control Situation

Romans 12:1-8 (NAS)

[1]I urge you therefore, brethren, by the mercies of God, to present your bodies a living and holy sacrifice, acceptable to God, which is your spiritual service of worship. [2]And do not be conformed to this world, but be transformed by the renewing of your mind, that you may prove what the will of God is, that which is good and acceptable and perfect. [3]For through the grace given to me I say to every man among you not to think more highly of himself than he ought to think; but to think so as to have sound judgment, as God has allotted to each a measure of faith. [4]For just as we have many members in one body and all the members do not have the same function, [5]so we, who are many, are one body in Christ, and individually members one of another. [6]And since we have gifts that differ according to the grace given to us, let each exercise them accordingly: if prophecy, according to the proportion of his faith; [7]if service, in his serving; or he who teaches, in his teaching; [8]or he who exhorts, in his exhortation; he who gives, with liberality; he who leads, with diligence; he who shows mercy, with cheerfulness.

1. Why was Rome "a control situation" for effective teaching on spiritual gifts? (pp. 129 and 132) ____

   _____

2. Identify two debatable issues surrounding why Paul wrote Romans and his knowledge of the Roman community. (pp. 129-131)
   (1) _____
   (2) _____

3. What factors belie the assumption that Corinthian-like gift problems existed in Rome? (p. 132) ____

   _____

4. How does Romans 12:1 tie together the two major sections of Romans? (p. 133) _____

   _____

5. How do the following words enhance the meaning of *sacrifice* in 12:1? (p. 134-135)
   living _____
   holy _____
   acceptable _____

6. What is a better translation of "spiritual service" in 12:1? (pp. 135-136) _____

7. How is the Christian mind renewed as described in 12:2? (p. 136) _____

8. How did grace (*charis*) legitimize and energize Paul's apostolic ministry? (pp. 137-138) _____

   _____

9. How is the role of grace even more apparent in the discussion of gifts in Romans than in 1 Corinthians? (p. 139) _____

_____

10. Describe the problems created in a church by overevaluation and underevaluation of self? (p. 140)

_____

_____

_____

11. Why is it important whether "measure of faith" in 12:3 pertains to quantity or individuality? (pp. 140-141) _____

_____

_____

12. Complete the following by filling in the missing words: "The entire process can be explained thus: having soberly _____ _____, the prophet is aware of his _____ potential: his gift, its _____, _____, and _____. He now must fully _____ his gift with the awareness that _____ _____ _____ _____ gift of _____. . . . (p. 142)

13. How does Paul's admonition to use gifts vary from prophecy to mercy? (p. 142) _____

_____

14. Why is the illustration of the body in 12:4-5 appropriate to the discussion of gifts? (p. 143) _____

_____

15. What was the primary purpose of the gift list in 12:6-8 if not to rank the gifts? (p. 144) _____

16. What are the two major categories of gifts in 12:6-8? (p. 144)
    (1) _____
    (2) _____

17. List the gifts mentioned in 12:6-8 and write a few words describing each. (pp. 144-146)
    (1) _____
    (2) _____
    (3) _____
    (4) _____
    (5) _____
    (6) _____
    (7) _____

18. If this gift list does not give insight into the community in Rome, what insight can be gained from it? (p. 146) _____
    _____
    _____

19. What are some possible reasons why Paul surrounded his teaching on gifts with ethical instruction? (pp. 147-148) _____
    _____
    _____

20. *Optional Activity:* Reproduce the table on p. 151. Rearrange the lists and try to match the thoughts that parallel.

7. Gifted Leaders Equipping Gifted Members

Ephesians 4:1-16

[1]I, therefore, the prisoner of the Lord, entreat you to walk in a manner worthy of the calling with which you have been called, [2]with all humility and gentleness, with patience, showing forbearance to one another in love, [3]being diligent to preserve the unity of the Spirit in the bond of peace. [4]There is one body and one Spirit, just as also you were called in one hope of your calling; [5]one Lord, one faith, one baptism, [6]one God and Father of all who is over all and through all and in all. [7]But to each one of us grace was given according to the measure of Christ's gift. [8]Therefore it says, "When He ascended on high, He led captive a host of captives, And He gave gifts to men." [9](Now this expression, "He ascended," what does it mean except that He also had descended into the lower parts of the earth? [10]He who descended is Himself also He who ascended far above all the heavens, that He might fill all things.) [11]And He gave some as apostles, and some as prophets, and some as evangelists, and some as pastors and teachers, [12]for the equipping of the saints for the work of service, to the building up of the body of Christ; [13]until we all attain to the unity of the faith, and of the knowledge of

the Son of God, to a mature man, to the measure of the stature which belongs to the fulness of Christ. [14]As a result, we are no longer to be children, tossed here and there by waves, and carried about by every wind of doctrine, by the trickery of men, by craftiness in deceitful scheming; [15]but speaking the truth in love, we are to grow up in all aspects into Him, who is the head, even Christ, [16]from whom the whole body, being fitted and held together by that which every joint supplies, according to the proper working of each individual part, causes the growth of the body fo the building up of itself in love.

1. What aspects of Ephesians draw into question Pauline authorship? (p. 154) _____

_____

2. What elements of Ephesians make it unlikely that the letter was addressed to a particular congregation? (pp. 154-155) _____

_____

3. What influence did the heretical teachings at Colossae have on Paul's decision to write the Ephesian letter? (p. 155) _____

_____

4. What role did Tychicus and Onesimus play in the letters to Colossae, Ephesus, and Philemon? (p. 156)

_____

_____

_____

5. Identify the churches that made up the "Christian mail route" of Asia Minor. (pp. 156-157)

   (1) _____

   (2) _____

   (3) _____

   (4) _____

   (5) _____

   (6) _____

   (7) _____

6. What is meant by a "circular letter"? (pp. 156-158)

   _____

   _____

   _____

7. What is the letter Paul mentioned in Colossians 4:16 as "my letter that is coming from Laodicea"? (p. 157)

   _____

8. Why is an understanding of the Colossian heresy important to a study of Ephesians? (pp. 158-159)

   _____

   _____

9. Identify four elements in the Colossian heresy. (pp. 158-159)

   (1) _____

   (2) _____

   (3) _____

   (4) _____

10. What was the "communication problem" Paul faced in writing Colossians and Ephesians? (p. 159) ____

    _____

    _____

11. What explanation does Dr. Hemphill give for the vacillation between prayer and teaching in Ephe-

sians 1—3? (p. 160) _____

12. How did Paul use the theme of Christ's authority and dominion over the universe to combat the Colossian heresy? (pp. 160-161) _____

13. How do we "play church"? (p. 161) _____

14. What truth, alluded to in 4:1, forms the basis for the requirements of Ephesians 4—6, and is the foundation for unity and mutual service in the church? (pp. 162-163) _____

15. How are the attributes mentioned in 4:2 produced in a believer's life? (p. 164) _____

16. Why is the gifted community of believers dependent on one another? (p. 166) _____

17. Identify the seven members mentioned in 4:4-6 as the sevenfold expression of unity and the role each plays in bringing unity to the body of Christ. (pp. 166-168)

    (1) _____

    (2) _____

    (3) _____

    (4) _____

    (5) _____

    (6) _____

(7) _____

18. How can unity in the body of Christ be both gift and goal? (p. 168) _____

_____

19. Why did Paul emphasize unity in his first letter to the Corinthians? (p. 168) _____

_____

to the Ephesians? (p. 168) _____

_____

20. Identify two meanings of the Greek word *charisma*. (p. 170) _____

_____

21. Why is every believer by nature charismatic in a true biblical sense? (p. 171) _____

_____

22. How has the term *charismatic* become a divisive dilemma instead of a unifying, edifying force in our churches today? (p. 171) _____

_____

23. Why was Paul's emphasis on Christ as the Giver of gifts a blow to the Colossian heresy? (pp. 172-173)

_____

_____

24. How is the triumph of Christ portrayed in 4:9-10? (pp. 173-174) _____

_____

25. What difference does it make to Paul's teaching on gifts whether the prepositional phrases in 4:12 are

coordinate or subordinate? (pp. 177-179) _____
_____
_____

26. Why do some scholars find the gift list in 4:11 troublesome? (p. 180) _____
_____
_____

27. How was the gift list in 4:11 peculiarly suited for Paul's readers? (pp. 181-182) _____
_____

28. Why is numbering the Pauline gifts a misunderstanding of the dynamic nature of Paul's teaching? (p. 183) _____
_____
_____

29. Why does a gifted believer still need to be equipped for service? (p. 185) _____
_____

30. In 4:13, what is the goal of full utilization of gifts? (pp. 188-189) _____
_____

31. What is the meaning of "the fulness of Christ" in 4:13? (pp. 188-189) _____
_____
_____

32. Contrast the behaviors/characteristics of the "mature man" and "children" as given in 4:13-15. (pp. 189-190)

MATURE MAN   *CHILDREN*

33. What words in 4:15 describe the sphere of the Christian life and the manner in which all Christian ministry is to take place? (pp. 190-191) _____

34. What four prominent themes does Paul summarize in 4:1-16? (pp. 191-192)

    (1) _____

    _____

    (2) _____

    _____

    (3) _____

    _____

    (4) _____

    _____

35. What unique emphasis is given in 4:1-16 related to proper use of gifts? (p. 195) _____

    _____

    _____

36. How does Ephesians challenge us? (p. 196) _____

    _____

    _____

8. Pulling It All Together

1. Write "Thessalonians," "Corinthians," "Romans," or "Ephesians" beside the statement that matches Paul's writing to that community. (pp. 198-199)

_____ Paul developed the central ideas of 1 Corinthians 12—14 but took them a step further to meet the challenge of heretical teaching.

_____ Paul emphasized the responsibility of all believers to minister for the common good but did not indicate that all believers were gifted.

_____ Paul synthesized his teaching on gifts in a clear and nonpolemic fashion.

_____ Paul insisted that all believers were gifted and declared that the manifestations of the Spirit were better understood as manifestations of God's graciousness.

2. Summarize seven truths that can be drawn from Paul's gift teaching. (p. 203)

(1) _____

(2) _____

(3) _____

(4) _____

(5) _____

(6) _____

(7) _____

3. Why are spiritual gifts and ethics related? (pp. 204-205) _____

   _____

4. What three elements does Dr. Hemphill suggest must be present in an authentic spiritual gift? (pp. 205-206)

   (1) _____

   (2) _____

   (3) _____

5. Where can we find a clue for discovering and developing our spiritual gift? (p. 207) _____

   _____

6. What happens to the value or meaning of a gift when taken out of the context of the church? (p. 208) _____

   _____

7. A spiritual gift is empowered by the Spirit of God only when recognized as a _____ gift, committed in _____ to the _____, and _____ exercised in _____ service to the _____. (p. 209)

8. Should charismatic activity (use of gifts) be controlled? _____ Why or why not? (pp. 209-210)

   _____

   _____

Appendix

Discovering My Gift

You may be wondering; "How do I go about discovering my gift? Just where do I begin? You've already made a significant beginning with your careful study of the important biblical texts on gifts. Let's take another step and consider several critical questions that may get you started on this lifelong process.

(A) You are not to think you must find your gift on some particular gift list put together by a compilation of those lists discussed in this book. God is infinitely creative and is still capable of granting new gifts for the work of ministry today. Many gifts, however, lie latent below the surface of the individual's consciousness and simply await discovery and development. Often a person will discover that what they have thought to be a natural talent is in truth a gift of God that can be energized by His Spirit. The Christian, at his/her new birth, receives the Spirit from God to know the things freely given to us by God (1 Cor. 2:12). God is the author of what the world calls "natural talents." When surrendered to Him, these talents are infused by His power and can rightly be called spiritual gifts. As such, they must be placed under His Lordship and used for service to the body.

Thus the first questions ask you what gift(s) you are already utilizing but have not identified as spiritual gifts.

1) What do you do well that encourages other believers? _____

2) In what areas of service do you find great satisfaction, fulfillment, and energy? _____

3) What ministry area do you get most enthusiastic and excited about? _____

4) Are there services that you perform that cause people to say: "You really do that well. You ministered to me?" _____

5) Has your pastor or other close, mature spiritual friend suggested areas of giftedness? ____ What were they? _____

6) If there were no limitations, to what area of ministry in your church would you be most inclined? ____

7) Have you sought any training to develop your gifts? (Remember the pastor/teacher is to equip the saints for the work of ministry - Eph. 4:11-12.) _____

8) Are you willing to be trained? _____

9) Are you willing to fully surrender the gifts identified above to the Lord's service through your church? _____

(B) Discovering New Gifts

It is possible that you are already exercising some gift(s) within the church but desire or need to develop other areas of giftedness. It's OK to be zealous for gifts, but we must follow the direction of Scripture: "So also you, since you are zealous of spiritual gifts, seek to abound for the edification of the church" (1 Cor. 14:12).

1) What is your motive for desiring a new spiritual gift? Be honest and ask the Spirit to search your heart. Is it solely to edify the body? _____

_____

_____

Then proceed . . .

2) Do you see needs in the church that aren't being met that cause you great concern? ____ What are they?

_____

_____

3) Have you been praying for a *particular* area of the church's ministry? ____ What area? _____

4) Do you have any abilities that could be leading you to serve in these ministries? _____

_____

If yes . . .

a) Would you be willing to surrender them to the Lordship of Christ right now and allow Him to fully empower them for His service? _____

b) Would you be willing to allow your pastor to provide further training in this area? _____ (gifts can be developed!)

c) Will you use it for the edification of the body?

_____

If no . . .

a) Ask the Holy Spirit to give you the ability you desire to meet the unique need that has burdened you. _____

_____

b) Share with your pastor and another mature friend about your desire and ask them to pray with you.

c) Ask if there is or can be training available to assist you in developing the gift that you are seeking.

d) Commit now to use your gift(s) solely for God's glory in service to His body.

C. In the exciting pilgrimage of discovering your gift(s) remember these five keys.

1) Seek Spiritual Discernment

Spiritual gifts can be abilities given by God before conversion that are now recognized and submitted to Him *or* they can be new abilities given to meet specific needs. Remember that we have received the Spirit of God "that we might know the things freely given to us by God" (1 Cor. 2:12).

Ask God to reveal your gift(s) for ministry.

2) Be willing to submit your gift(s) to the Lordship of Christ.

When you commit your gift to His Lordship, it is His to do with as He wills. Bring your gift under the authority of your church's leadership. This will bring the body's validation and confirmation.

3) Use your gift in the context of the body of Christ. All gifts are given for the common good. Ask your church leadership to help you become involved in the ministries of the church.

4) Since you are zealous for spiritual gifts, seek to abound for the good of the body.
5) Remain open to training for the full development of your gifts to the glory of God.